Written by Rachel Elliot
Illustrated by Xuân Thanh Lê

First published 2016 by Parragon Books, Ltd.
Copyright © 2019 Cottage Door Press, LLC
5005 Newport Drive, Rolling Meadows, Illinois 60008
All Rights Reserved

10 9 8 7 6 5 4 3 2 1

ISBN 978-1-68052-515-1

Parragon Books is an imprint of Cottage Door Press, LLC.
Parragon Books® and the Parragon® logo are
registered trademarks of Cottage Door Press, LLC.

The EASTER STORY

PaRragon.

It was a very exciting day in Jerusalem. Riding on a humble donkey, Jesus had arrived in the city for the Festival of Passover. Cheers rang out from the crowd and palm leaves waved in the air. Everyone had come to see their king entering the city.

"God bless the king who comes in the name of the Lord!"

they shouted. "Hosanna in the highest!"

Many people laid palm leaves down for the donkey to walk upon.

Everyone wanted to show their love and respect.

Jesus went straight to the city's temple, where he got a terrible shock. In the temple's courtyard, people were buying goods, changing money, and selling animals. It was noisy and smelly. The air was filled with the shouts of sellers and the cries of animals. Jesus felt anger rise up inside him.

"The house of God is a house of prayer," he roared. "But you have turned it into a den of greed!"

He turned over the tables of goods, and coins rained down to the ground. The sellers scurried away, making room for people to pray. Jesus's supporters cheered, but the chief priests were furious.

"He wants to destroy our power over the people," they snarled.

The priests controlled people by making them afraid, but people listened to Jesus because he talked about love.

"If only we could get rid of him," the priests muttered.

Six days before the Festival of Passover, Jesus and his disciples went to stay with some friends. They were served a special meal and, while they relaxed around the table, a woman opened a jar of expensive perfumed oil. She kneeled down and rubbed the oil onto Jesus's feet, then wiped them with her hair.

"You could have sold that and given the money to the poor," snapped Judas, one of Jesus's disciples.

"Leave her alone," said Jesus. "She is being kind."

But Judas felt angry with Jesus, and his anger allowed evil to creep into his heart. He knew that the chief priests didn't like Jesus, and he decided to help them get rid of him. Two days before Passover, he met with them and agreed to lead them to Jesus when Jesus was alone.

"I will kiss Jesus to show the guards who to arrest," he told the priests. In return, the priests promised to pay Judas thirty pieces of silver.

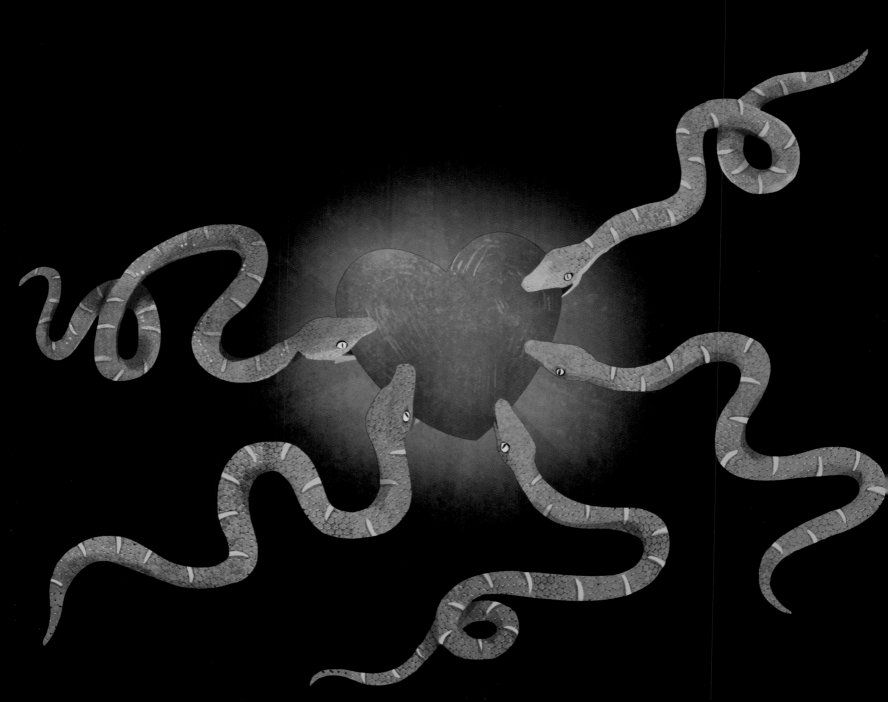

Jesus knew that the priests were plotting against him. He also knew that it was all part of God's plan, and that he would leave the world soon to join his Father in heaven. But he still felt sad when he thought about what was going to happen.

The evening before Passover, Jesus took some water and kneeled in front of each of the twelve disciples in turn. He gently washed their feet and dried them on a towel.

"Lord, you should not wash our feet," said the disciples. "You are too important."

"No one is more important than anyone else," Jesus said. "Even though I am your teacher, we are all equal, because we are all God's children."

On the day of Passover, Jesus and his disciples sat down to eat a special meal together.

"Soon, one of you will betray me," Jesus told them. The disciples were shocked—all except Judas.

"Who is it?" they asked. "Who could do this?"

But Jesus would not speak Judas's name. He blessed the bread by saying a prayer, then broke it into pieces and handed it to his disciples.

"Like this bread, my body will be broken," he said. "Please eat it."

He blessed the wine and passed around the cup, so they could all drink from it, to show they were part of God's family.

"This wine is like my blood, which will be spilled for many people," he said. "Please drink it."

As they ate and drank, Jesus watched his disciples with sadness in his heart.

"Eat and drink to remember me," he said. "We won't have another meal together until we are in God's kingdom."

There was a quiet garden called Gethsemane, where Jesus liked to pray. After the meal, he took Peter, James, and John there to pray with him. While they rested, Jesus fell to his knees to pray. He knew that the priests were coming for him, and he felt afraid.

"Father, I know what needs to happen, but it's going to be very hard," he said. "Please help me."

Jesus spoke to God for a long time and his disciples fell asleep.

Soon, Judas entered the garden. Judas was followed by men armed with swords and fiery torches.

"Rise!" Jesus called. "Here comes the traitor."

Peter, James, and John rose quickly, but it was too late. Judas walked up to Jesus and kissed his cheek. It was his signal to the guards that this was the man to arrest. The guards grabbed Jesus by the arms and held him tightly. Peter wanted to fight, but Jesus stopped him.

"My Father in heaven will protect me," he said.

Early the next morning, the chief priests took Jesus to Pontius Pilate, the Roman governor. The Romans were in charge of Jerusalem, so it was Pilate's job to decide what would happen to prisoners.

Pilate questioned Jesus, trying to find out if Jesus was an enemy of Rome. He knew that the chief priests wanted Jesus dead, but he believed Jesus was harmless.

By that time, a large crowd had gathered.

"Do you want me to release the King of the Jews?" Pilate asked them.

The chief priests had already talked to the crowd and told them lies about Jesus.

"No!" the people shouted. "Crucify him!"

"Why?" Pilate asked. "What crime has he committed?"

But the crowd just kept shouting, "Crucify him!"

Pilate was a weak man and he wanted to please the people. So he had Jesus beaten and then handed him over to be crucified.

The soldiers dressed Jesus in a purple robe to make fun of him. Purple was the color that kings wore, and they thought he had been pretending to be a king. They mocked him and laughed at him. They even twisted together some thorns to make a crown and placed it on his head.

"Hail, King of the Jews!" they shouted, laughing at him.

Jesus was forced to carry a heavy, wooden cross through the crowded city streets. All the way, people jeered and shouted at him. It was very different from the way he had arrived in Jerusalem.

At nine o'clock in the morning, the soldiers nailed Jesus to the cross.

"Father, forgive them," Jesus whispered. "They don't understand what they are doing."

The minutes crept by like hours and Jesus was in great pain. It became harder and harder for him to breathe. A crowd gathered, shouting nasty things at Jesus and making fun of him.

"If you were really the son of God, you would save yourself," they jeered. "Come down from the cross!"

Jesus did not reply. He felt as if each breath was tearing at his body. The sun shrank away, and the sky became dark and stormy, but the crowd and the priests kept shouting their cruel words.

Finally, at three o'clock, with a loud cry, the son of God took his last breath.

Later that day, a Roman named Joseph took down Jesus's body, wrapped it in linen and placed it in a tomb. Then, he rolled a large, heavy stone over the entrance.

Early the next morning, Mary Magdalene, one of Jesus's friends, came to visit the tomb. To her amazement, she found that the large stone had been rolled away.

Mary stepped into the dark tomb and saw that Jesus's body was gone. All that was left were the strips of linen in which he had been wrapped.

"He is not here," said a voice.

Mary turned and saw a man dressed all in white. He was an angel, but she did not know that. She gasped in fear.

"Do not be afraid," the man said. "Jesus has risen! Go, tell his disciples."

Trembling with shock and overcome with happiness, Mary fled from the tomb and ran to find Peter and John.

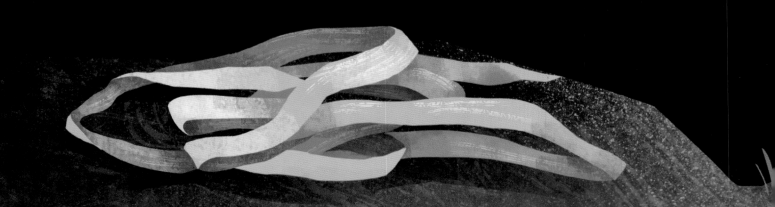

At first, Peter and John did not believe Mary's story. They followed her to the tomb and ran inside.

"Someone has stolen the body!" they cried. "Who could have done such a thing?"

They went to tell the other disciples what had happened, but Mary stayed behind.

"What shall I do?" she cried, tears running down her face.

She was afraid to be there alone, but she did not want to go home, either.

"Mary," said a familiar voice.

She knew Jesus's voice at once. But how could it be him? A man stepped forward.

"Master!" Mary cried, falling to her knees before him.

"Tell the disciples what you have seen," said Jesus. "I will soon be with my Father in heaven."

Mary ran back to find the disciples.

"I have seen my Lord with my own eyes," she cried. "He has risen from the grave!"

Over the next forty days, Jesus appeared many times to his disciples. On the Mount of Olives, near Jerusalem, he spoke to them one last time.

"It is time for me to return to my Father in heaven," he said. "Everything has happened just as He said it would. But I will always be with you."

The sun burst out from behind a bank of clouds. As golden beams of light dazzled them, the disciples watched Jesus rise up to heaven. Then, two angels appeared, dressed in shimmering white.

"Jesus will come back to you," they promised.

The disciples shared smiles of love and happiness. They knew that, until Jesus returned, they would keep his words alive. They would spread his message of love throughout the world.